GW00602758

ASTROLOGY GEMS

LEO

July 23 – August 22

Monte Farber & Amy Zerner

Sterling Publishing Co., Inc.
New York

Text © 2006 by Monte Farber
Art © 2006 by Amy Zerner

10 9 8 7 6 5 4 3 2 1

Published by Sterling Publishing Co., Inc.

387 Park Avenue South, New York, NY 10016

Distributed in Canada by Sterling Publishing
c/o Canadian Manda Group, 165 Dufferin Street
Toronto, Ontario, Canada M6K 3H6

Distributed in the United Kingdom by GMC
Distribution Services
Castle Place, 166 High Street, Lewes, East Sussex,
England BN7 1XU

Distributed in Australia by Capricorn Link (Australia)
Pty. Ltd.
P.O. Box 704, Windsor, NSW 2756, Australia

Printed in China

Sterling ISBN-13: 978-1-4027-4180-7
          ISBN-10: 1-4027-4180-4

For information about custom editions, special sales,
premium and corporate purchases, please contact
Sterling Special Sales Department at 800-805-5489 or
specialsales@sterlingpub.com.

What's Your Sign?

When someone asks you "What's your sign?" you know what that person really means is "What's your astrological sign?" Professional astrologers more often use the phrase "Sun sign," a term reflecting the concept that a person's sign is determined by which of the twelve signs of the zodiac the Sun appeared to be passing through at the moment she was born. The zodiac is the narrow band of sky circling the Earth's equator through which the Sun, the Moon, and the planets appear to move when viewed by us here on Earth.

Astrology's Gift

Astrology, which has been around for thousands of years, is the study of how planetary positions relate to earthly events and people. Its long and rich history has resulted in a wealth of philosophical and psychological wisdom, the basic concepts of which we are going to share with you in the pages of this book. As the Greek philosopher Heracleitus (c. 540–c. 480 BCE) said, "Character is destiny." Who you are— complete with all of your goals, tenden- cies, habits, virtues, and vices—will

determine how you act and react, thereby creating your life's destiny. Like astrology itself, our Astrology Gems series is designed to help you to better know yourself and those you care about. You will then be better able to use your free will to shape your life to your liking.

Does Astrology Work?

Many people rightly question how astrology can divide humanity into twelve Sun signs and make predictions that can be correct for everyone of the same sign. The simple answer is that it cannot do that—that's newspaper astrology, entertaining but not the real thing. Rather, astrology can help you understand your strengths and weaknesses so that you can better accept yourself as you are and use your strengths to compensate for your weaknesses. Real astrology is designed to help you to become yourself fully.

Remember, virtually all the music in the history of Western music has been composed using variations of the same twelve notes. Similarly, the twelve Sun signs of astrology are basic themes rich with meaning that each of us expresses differently to create and respond to the unique opportunities and challenges of our life.

LEO

July 23–August 22

Planet
Sun

Element
Fire

Quality
Fixed

Day
Sunday

Season
summer

Colors
gold, orange, yellow

Plants
marigold, sunflower, nasturtium

Perfume
orange blossom

Gemstones
amber, carnelian, citrine, ruby

Metal
gold

Personal qualities
Creative, dramatic, proud, organized, and romantic

We call the following words "key-words" because they can help you unlock the core meaning of the astrological sign of Leo. Each key-word represents issues and ideas that are of supreme importance and prominence in the lives of people born with Leo as their Sun sign. You will usually find that every Leo embodies at least one of these keywords in the way he makes a living:

self-assertion · creativity
a place in the Sun · recognition
theatricality · hobbies
leadership · romance · pleasures
fun · hospitality · appreciation
openheartedness · beach resorts
fame · playfulness · children
entertainment · luck · gambling
sports · acting out · games
performance · sun worshipping
love affair · regal bearing
self-love · hero or heroine
prizewinner · golden objects
show business

Leo's Symbolic Meaning

Leo is the sign of the creative organizers of the zodiac. Practically no one is as good as they are at recognizing the solution to a problem and organizing the means to solve it. It is this ability that gives rise to Leo's reputation as a great leader. Like all leaders, most Leos feel more comfortable when they are telling others what has to be done rather than taking care of the routine details themselves. They get annoyed with themselves for this trait, but not for long, because Leos like themselves a lot. They put themselves where there is much that needs to be done and they associate themselves with the right group of people so that their creative input is always welcome, even if they do not always jump in and get their hands dirty.

The symbol for Leo is the strong and proud male lion, a most appropriate symbol. Not only is a group of lions referred to as a "pride," but also the importance of personal pride to those born during the time of Leo cannot be overstated. They do not want to be connected to anyone or anything that they do not feel is up to their high personal standards.

Showing us all how things are done is a special gift that Leos possess. This is why they have such a knack for drama—acting, the arts and music, or any form of display. Their generosity requires them to create situations and objects that will benefit and entertain them and those they consider worthy to be connected with them.

Leo is one of the four Fixed Sun signs of astrology (the other three are Taurus, Scorpio, and Aquarius). Fixed signs are stable, resolute, and determined. They represent the force of holding steady. Being a Fixed sign makes Leos loyal, stubborn, and proud.

Leo is also a Fire sign, one of three (Aries and Sagittarius are the other two). Fire signs are primarily energetic, enthusiastic, and impulsive.

Leos are legendary for their ability to help and protect those who acknowledge them as special people. They gain a sense of their own self-worth by giving what they think others need from them. However, it is important that they remember that they, too, need help and protection. Leos are usually too prideful to ask for help.

Recognizing a Leo

People who exhibit the physical characteristics distinctive of the sign Leo look noble. They may seem tall and possess a majestic countenance. A Leo knows how to dress to impress. Leo's inner sense of royalty exudes dignity, elegance, and class. A Leo's hair can appear to be like a lion's mane—a feature of pride that catches the attention of others. Leos move with a natural athletic grace.

Leo's Typical Behavior and Personality Traits

- needs to be admired
- trusting and loyal
- uses charm to get what she wants
- likes to show off
- trusting
- likes excitement
- generous

- has elegant tastes
- popular
- gives and expects respect
- generous with affection
- is a leader

What Makes a Leo Tick?

Leos may worry that they are not as proud, powerful, or good a leader as they wish they were, and that people who matter to them will discover this fact. At times they need to fall back on the "fake it till you make it" philosophy. Sometimes, even the best of leaders must put on an act to get the job done. Leos find it very difficult to be a team player, since they feel it is their lot to lead others.

The Leo Personality Expressed Positively

At their very best, Leos are an intelligent, creative force wherever they operate. Their ability to solve problems with a combination of optimism and common sense is a marvel to behold. Leos have a rare talent for being both commanding and friendly at the same time. When Leo is happy, he makes the whole world around him a bit sunnier.

On a Positive Note

Leos displaying the positive characteristics associated with their sign also tend to be:

- ❀ attractive and demonstrative
- ❀ positive thinking
- ❀ dignified and charming
- ❀ honest and loyal
- ❀ proud of their homes
- ❀ warm, friendly, and generous with gifts
- ❀ courageous and bold
- ❀ responsible and mature
- ❀ adoring of loved ones

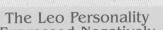

The Leo Personality Expressed Negatively

When Leos are working on projects for others to look at, their audience's feedback becomes very important to them. If their creations are not acknowledged or praised to the hilt, their pride will be hurt. As a result, they might forget their usual kindhearted ways and may even try to use their power or influence to sway the opinions of others. They may sulk if attention is not paid to them or to their efforts.

Negative Traits

Leos displaying the negative characteristics associated with their sign also tend to be:

- ❋ superior in attitude

- ❋ status conscious

- ❋ smug and conceited

- ❋ arrogant and self-involved

- ❋ stubborn or willful

- ❋ overdramatic

- ❋ brooding and vengeful

- ❋ judgmental about appearances

- ❋ overeager to impress

Ask a Leo If...

Ask a Leo if you need help organizing a project or enterprise of any sort. The task can be big or small, complicated or relatively easy, but no matter what it is, Leo has a plan for how to get it done better, faster, more economically, and even with more style. She believes that her way is the only way, and will probably tell you so. Leo may criticize your way of handling things, but always in a pleasing manner!

Leos As Friends

Leos as friends are caring, thoughtful, warm, and fun to be with. They love their friends and need to feel proud of them. They are generous with resources and hospitality, expecting friends to show their gratitude in kind. Leos dislike cheapness in any form and are unlikely to make friends with people whom they perceive as being cheap. In general, Leos like their friends to be successful, but not so successful as to take any attention away from Leo's limelight! A friend who has strong personal aspirations or ambitions that compete with Leo's may find it impossible to have a close and trusting relationship.

A friend who fails a Leo by criticizing something she has done or belittling something she cares deeply about may be dropped like a hot potato.

Looking for Love

Leos need to put themselves into the most positive situations to find love. If they are in a place where they are happy, they will create an incredible relationship. If they are in a place where their energy has to be used just to keep things going, they could lose one of their most valuable possessions: their time. If a Leo does not have a good relationship, the reason most likely has to do with ego. The Leo may be too concerned with status to be able to be with people who are good for her. To Leo, love is a dramatic ideal, and sometimes this factor overshadows the possibility of romance with someone who may not look, act, or seem like someone Leo believes she should be with. Leos are not shallow people, but they do set the bar very high. Male Leos seem to have no trouble attracting women, while female Leos attract many men with their natural beauty and liveliness.

Leos don't endorse the "friends first, lovers later" philosophy. They are often likely to fall in love at first sight, or at least on the first date! For them, romance is more likely to flower from a chance meeting, by coincidence, or through paths crossed by accident. It is common for Leos to transfer all their ideas and ideals about romance to a new love affair, believing that the one they have fallen in love with possesses all the traits and characteristics they desire, even if this isn't the case. In fact, the biggest disappointment Leos in love can suffer is to discover that the one they love isn't the paragon of romantic virtues they first envisioned.

Finding That Special Someone

Leos have to take the lead to create and improve and create the kind of relationship they want; they should not expect to simply sit back and let things happen. It would be good for a Leo to keep things organized and moving in terms of making dates and plans.

First Dates

The perfect first date for Leo can be attending a sporting event or going to a movie. Leos don't need the quiet intimacy of a dimly lit restaurant to create a spirit of emotional intimacy and romance. They love to be in the midst of a crowd. They are often movie buffs as well, so an evening spent watching a new comedy over popcorn could also be their style.

Leos are active people, and they enjoy being out in the sunshine, so a good first date could be sailing, surfing, or just lying in the sun. A stroll on the beach at sunset sets a romantic mood.

Leo in Love

Leos are the true romantics of the zodiac. They can enjoy all kinds of fun things and creative expressions together with their partners. It is rewarding for a Leo to actively pursue creative projects with a love interest. Attending creative classes together, visiting museums, and going to art galleries, movies, dance recitals, concerts, and the theater are all pursuits that light a Leo's fire. A long vacation is also a perfect way to stimulate Leo's romantic nature.

Undying Love

For Leo, problems in a relationship may be the result of not making time for fun and romance. Children may be the problem, or views on children may conflict, especially regarding the conditions that have to be present before children can be brought into the world and reared properly. Trouble in a Leo's relationships could also be caused by problems related to organization, responsibility, and leadership. If Leo finds that there are many essential tasks that neither partner is good at, then both must try their best to do them together.

Expectations in Love

Leo wants a partner who enhances her own image and who enjoys being in the spotlight as much as she does. Leo's partner must be good-looking and have great taste, but should not detract attention from Leo. Leo wants a partner who will place her on a pedestal and believe in her dreams with all of his heart. Leo loves good manners, expects to be treated like royalty, and needs total commitment of faithfulness and adoration from a loved one. Affection is an important factor in any Leo relationship. Leos need to be shown in all ways that they are loved.

Leo's partner must enjoy all aspects of entertaining and must have the creative flair for making their home a beautiful showcase. With the right partner, a Leo will rise in social status due to her generous hospitality, enthusiasm, and persistence for excellence. Consequently, Leo's fire will make her partner shine, too. Despite having a large ego, Leo is dedicated to being the ideal partner, too.

What Leos Look For

Because appearance and style mean a lot to Leo, these may often be the first things he searches for in a romantic partner. But there are many other traits that are important to him, so he is not likely to judge on looks alone. Leos require someone whose enthusiasm and zest for life matches their own. They are not interested in people who are emotional downers or too needy, no matter how attractive they might otherwise be. Healthy self-esteem is a trait Leos admire in others.

If Leo Only Knew...

If Leo only knew that even the greatest ruler has to listen to the advice of others. An unrestrained ego can do more damage to Leo and her creations than any enemy. Leos need to realize that they cannot always be the star of the show and that there are times when it is better for them to follow the example of others rather than always having to lead the way. They should know that it is not only their masterful personality but also their sunniness, kind disposition, and fair-minded approach to life that attracts the admiration and love of the people around them.

Marriage

Leos and their partners should create projects together that have a life of their own, such as business enterprises, or works of art, such as tapestries, plays, sculpture, novels, clothing, movies, music, and other similar things. One of the most creative things people can produce is a child, and Leos love children. Just being connected with children and things related to them brings Leos much joy. Add to that the previously mentioned businesses and artistic enterprises, and even material benefits can result.

No matter how busy a Leo is, she must make time for romantic interludes. A relationship where there is no romance is in danger of ending.

Leo's Opposite Sign

Aquarius, the Water Carrier, is the complementary opposite sign of Leo. There may be tough relations between them, but Aquarius can show Leo how to share without needing appreciation, and how to give the center stage to others. This can be a big challenge for Leo, but it is a way in which he can learn to stand alone and value himself. Aquarius does not approach life from Leo's sunny perspective, and in this way, the Lion can be a good example for Aquarius to copy.

Pairing Up

In general, if people display the characteristics typical of their sign, intimate relationships between a Leo and another individual can be described as follows:

Leo with Leo
Harmonious, so long as both are willing to share the spotlight

Leo with Virgo
Harmonious, but personality differences need a wide berth

Leo with Libra
Harmonious; the equivalent of a lifelong party

Leo with Scorpio
Difficult, since both are equally
stubborn

Leo with Sagittarius
Harmonious, as friends as well
as lovers

Leo with Capricorn
Turbulent, if Capricorn won't
relinquish the purse strings

Leo with Aquarius
Difficult, but the partners are able to
illuminate life lessons for each other

Leo with Pisces
Turbulent, if Pisces can't stand up to
Leo's demands

Leo with Aries
Harmonious; a lifelong romance and undying passion

Leo with Taurus
Difficult, but with deeply sensual overtones

Leo with Gemini
Harmonious; a partnership of ideas as well as romance

Leo with Cancer
Harmonious, if differences bring out the best in each other

If Things Don't Work Out

The partner who is unfaithful to Leo, or who walks out on a serious love affair, will leave behind a very wounded person. It will take Leo months to recover from such a deep hurt and may make him very wary of risking serious love again. Leo will need to heal not only a broken heart, but a broken spirit as well. A love affair that ends badly can greatly impact Leo's ego and self-esteem.

Leo at Work

It is good for a Leo to be creative, no matter what her job or career. This always requires her to look at what projects and tasks she tackles in a new way. A Leo should not just accept that she knows the best way to accomplish a goal at work. It is very important that a Leo does work that allows her to somehow express her ability to create solutions to problems and general improvements. Leo could even try to bring in someone, maybe even a young person, and explain the problem to him. The fresh look of his eyes may provide a surprising solution.

Although Leo has the ability to work as an effective team member, she doesn't necessarily have the temperament for it. She is accustomed to being the "idea person" on projects, as well as the dynamic force that gets the project done. Also, it is difficult for Leo to abdicate the role as authority figure, harder still to admit learning a better way of doing things from someone else. Other than creative input, Leo's best attribute in the workplace is a genius for organization.

Typical Occupations

A job in traditionally creative fields such as music, dance, acting, writing, design, or fashion would be wonderful for a Leo. Leos possess a strong creative and dramatic personality, and you will find many in the theater, television, and film industry. They become stars of stage or screen, talented musicians, or well-known painters, so a career opportunity in the arts could be pursued. Other jobs that may be good for Leo are investing, sports-related work, gaming of all kinds, and opportunities to display goods, either for ads or in the place where they are sold. Leos may also find that they are called on to do some public speaking, another opportunity to display their innate creativity.

Leos do well in careers where they can rise to the top. In the political arena, they keep going until they reach a powerful position. In business, you can find Leo as chairperson or president or on the board of directors. Leos are ambitious by nature, and prefer to take charge and delegate. Many Leos go into business for themselves.

Details, Details

Because Leos' chief ability is leadership, it may be believed that they can't handle the details of a project, but this isn't the case. It is precisely because they are so good at balancing the importance of details with an ability to see the whole picture that they are successful. However, even though they make use of details in an admirable way, they can show disdain for them if they get in the way of a larger concept.

Leos can also be quite creative in work that requires physical labor. They don't believe in cutting corners and always adhere to the prescribed guidelines or safety standards. Leo often shows her inner strength when under the pressures of a deadline or crisis. Even in the most chaotic, stressful, and messy situations, Leo's ability to keep track of detailed information and use it to the best possible advantage shows just how helpful her organizational skills can be.

Time management is a Leo specialty. Leos are especially prolific leading a team effort that is deadline sensitive. Because of their natural leadership ability and gift for prioritizing tasks, Leos prove that to be detail oriented does not mean being shortsighted!

Behavior and Abilities at Work

In the workplace, the typical Leo:

* must be in charge

* makes a good impression

* has many talents

* gives wonderful speeches

* can't admit mistakes

* likes to dress the part

Leo As Employer

A typical Leo boss:

❄ can create enthusiasm for a project

❄ cannot tolerate tardiness or failure

❄ is charming and gives compliments

❄ cannot have his authority under-mined

❄ is generous with time and money

❄ takes the credit for successes

❄ instills confidence and devotion

❄ has a huge ego

❄ knows how to get the job done

Leo As Employee

A typical Leo employee:

* responds to genuine praise

* is very loyal and trustworthy

* needs to have his work recognized

* likes to prove that he is the best

* works hard to be promoted

* can create a congenial atmosphere

* likes to show off success

Leo As Coworker

Leos needs to be involved with people and in projects where they are able to use their leadership qualities. Whatever their job, they make sure they steal the limelight, which sometimes causes rifts with coworkers, even though they naturally get along well with others. Leos love to display pictures of places they have traveled, or of them at a memorable event. They need to inspire admiration, so they often display status symbols as well.

Money

Leos can benefit from taking calculated risks in the stock market and other legal forms of gambling, or from taking a chance on a new idea that comes as a creative inspiration. A Leo's good fortune can best come through having fun, enjoying love and romance, and being creative. If a Leo can look at even his routine tasks as pleasurable, it will bring into his life wealth and success in the fastest time possible.

Games, including sports, performing, creativity, and children, can benefit a Leo financially. A Leo is also in a very good position to profit, not only from all these things, but also from taking a chance on a calculated risk or gamble. Investing, a more socially respectable form of gambling, is also favored. Leos enjoy spending lavishly and would be wise to keep to a strict budget most of the time.

At Home

Leo sees his home as his castle. Lavishing attention on its care, beautifying it, as well as showing it off to others are his ways of showing what it means to him.

Every Leo has at least one object at home that others might consider ostentatious. A Leo needs to be able to be comfortable and completely herself at home and will get anxious to the degree that this is not possible.

Behavior and Abilities at Home

Leo typically:

✳ is able to complete household odd jobs

✳ is king of his castle

✳ shows strength of character in emergencies

✳ offers comfort and affection to family

✳ has a taste for elegance in the home

✳ needs others to respect his space

Leisure
Interests

Leos derive much benefit from allowing their creativity free rein. The rewards given to true artists are secondary in importance to the pleasure they get just from taking the time to make their art. Leos need to exercise their creative talents, in whatever manner they enjoy.

The typical Leo enjoys the following pastimes:

- watching competitive sports on TV
- reading celebrity biographies
- shopping for clothes
- keeping a journal
- going to concerts
- giving parties at home

Leo Likes

- a lot of action
- adoration and recognition
- being creative
- receiving gifts of gold
- famous people
- the theater
- an appreciative audience
- children and pets
- exotic food and restaurants
- warm places
- designer clothes

Leo Dislikes

* not being appreciated
* cold weather
* physical inactivity
* being ignored or not being chosen
* working behind the scenes
* cheap perfume
* being taken for granted
* being told she can't do something
* tacky furnishings
* eating every meal at home
* subtlety or subterfuge

The Secret Side of Leo

Privately, the typical Leo craves love more than anyone would ever guess. A true Leo is a person who wants to be on top, to be the one in charge, and to be listened to, without question. Yet, both the aspiration as well as the reality put great stress on Leo. While typical Leos may appear to be confident, especially when they take center stage, they have secret doubts about their true worth and may seriously undervalue themselves.

The Sun ☉

The sign Leo is ruled by the planet the
Sun. Though Sumerian and Babylonian
astrologers knew that the Sun was a star,
they counted it as a planet, the most
important one. The ancient astrological
symbol for the Sun, a dot in the center of
a circle, shows they knew that the Sun was
orbited by the planets. It also symbolizes
us in the center of our personal "solar
system" of friends, family, coworkers, and
neighbors. The Sun gives light and life
to our world, and in astrology the Sun

symbolizes the ego. The planets revolve around the Sun, which is why it also rules celebrity, status, and the power to reign. The Sun's heat and light give life, and so the Sun represents fatherhood in a warm, giving, illuminating sense. It represents a father who gives life to his offspring, believes in the abilities of his creations, and is proud of them. The Sun rules our hearts.

Bringing Up a Young Leo

Most little Leos have turbulent emotions and often act out in dramatic ways. They always enjoy the limelight at school and often take the lead in tasks and activities.

The friendly Leo nature endears Leo children to everyone, including strangers. Since they are generally outgoing, they need to be taught discernment when it comes to talking to strangers.

Parents may find a bossy little Leo on their hands if they don't use enough discipline and convincing to impress the importance of homework and doing jobs around the house. It is good to reward a Leo, as she needs plenty of love, hugs, and praise for her achievements.

She should also be taught to handle her allowance, as she is likely to spend it frivolously at times. As it is in almost all things with a young Leo, what is taught is not as important as what caregivers and other teachers demonstrate in their interactions with adults. Leo children have an innate knowledge that what people say and what they do are often two different things. Young Leos can become surprisingly comfortable with and adept at stretching the truth to suit their purposes if the adults around them fail to demonstrate that duplicitous behavior whose purpose is the avoiding of hurt feelings is the only proper use of not telling the truth.

Leo children are naturally happiest when doing something physical. As they grow up, they will be attracted to the opposite sex, get huge crushes, and fall in and out of love. A parent of any Leo needs to understand that Leos can be overdramatic, especially about romance, so they should encourage them to tell the truth.

Leo As a Parent

The typical Leo parent:

- ❄ is encouraging and approachable
- ❄ allows children to make messes
- ❄ likes organizing children's activities
- ❄ encourages children to play sports
- ❄ is liberal with discipline
- ❄ expresses affection easily and often

The Leo Child

The typical Leo child:

* does not like to sit still

* tries to be the center of attention

* loves games and playacting

* has a lot of energy

* is sunny and friendly

* is adventuresome and brave

* enjoys being catered to

* is generous with playmates

❀ dislikes being ignored

❀ loves parties and group endeavors

❀ is interested in romance from an early age

❀ will try to direct the actions of other children

❀ can sometimes stretch the truth a bit

❀ likes to pretend to be a parent or an authority

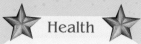

Health

Typical Leos are happy, healthy, energetic people as long as they are loved. If for some reason they are not getting the attention or affection that they crave, Leos will complain. They can sometimes overindulge in rich food and wine, but too much of this is bad. Care should be taken when it comes to putting on weight. Leos should take care of their hearts and backs, as these are the parts of the body that Leo rules.

Whatever physical
weaknesses he has, a typical
Leo will enjoy only a brief period
of rest before he is up again and on
the go. To be out of commission for
long is intolerable to a Leo.

✦ Famous Leos ✦

Ben Affleck

Tori Amos

Lucille Ball

Napoleon Bonaparte

Fidel Castro

Bill Clinton

Robert De Niro

Amelia Earhart

Henry Ford

Melanie Griffith

Alfred Hitchcock

Dustin Hoffman

Iman

Mick Jagger

Carl Jung

Jennifer Lopez

Madonna

Jacqueline Kennedy Onassis

Maxwell Parrish

Robert Redford

J.K. Rowling

Arnold Schwarzenegger

James Taylor

Charlize Theron

Andy Warhol

About the Authors

Internationally known self-help author Monte Farber's inspiring guidance and empathic insights impact everyone he encounters. Amy Zerner's exquisite one-of-a-kind spiritual couture creations and collaged fabric paintings exude her profound intuition and deep connection with archetypal stories and healing energies. Together, they have built The Enchanted World of Amy Zerner and Monte Farber: books, card decks, and

oracles that have helped millions discover their own spiritual paths.

Their best-selling titles include The Chakra Meditation Kit, The Enchanted Tarot, The Instant Tarot Reader, The Psychic Circle, Karma Cards, The Truth Fairy, The Healing Deck, True Love Tarot, Animal Powers Meditation Kit, The Breathe Easy Deck, The Pathfinder Psychic Talking Board, and Gifts of the Goddess Affirmation Cards.

For further information, please visit:
www.TheEnchantedWorld.com